T0328363

Tastes of Nature

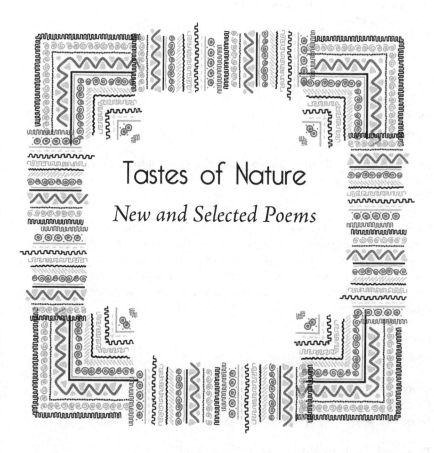

Tastes of Nature

New and Selected Poems

Ekpe Inyang

SPEARS BOOKS
Denver, Colorado

SPEARS BOOKS
AN IMPRINT OF SPEARS MEDIA PRESS LLC
7830 W. Alameda Ave, Suite 103-247
Denver, CO 80226
United States of America

First Published in the United States of America in 2022 by Spears Books
www.spearsmedia.com
info@spearsmedia.com
@spearsbooks

Information on this title: www.spearsmedia.com/tastes-of-nature
© 2022 Ekpe Inyang
All rights reserved.

ISBN: 9781957296005 (Paperback)
Also available in Kindle format

Cover photo: Antonio Solano
Cover designed by Doh Kambem
Designed and typeset by Spears Media Press LLC

Distributed globally by African Books Collective (ABC)
www.africanbookscollective.com

To my children and grandchildren and to children and grandchildren all over the world.

Contents

❖❖❖

PART THREE: THE DIALOGUE BEGINS

PART FOUR: NATURE IN TURMOIL

PART FIVE: PUTTING IT BACK RIGHT

FOREWORD

The ideology of late modernity taught us to apply a global perspective to the world. "Place" was dissolved in "space", the traditional borders of nations, cultures, and languages replaced by the free flow of goods, resources, and people. This was a world without limits and limitations, a global village of diminishing distances. The ruling metaphors for this conceptual transformation were the network and the global marketplace.

Most importantly, the "globe" of globalization was a world of abstraction. It was neither the Gaia nor Mother Earth of mythical thinking – a "primitive" notion now rendered obsolete – nor the "Blue Marble" of science, with its planetary perspective of Earth as an actual, physical object. Most fundamentally, this abstract globe was a vast yet intangible forum of infinite virtual exchange. Nature had no place in a world which sought to do away with everything tangible and localized, all things rooted in the soil of materiality. To use a simile from the present collection of poetry, the global discourse took place on "the stage of monologue", reducing the "great dialogue" between Nature and Culture to a meaningless monotony. Yet although we stopped listening to the voice of Nature, our own words continued to exert a violent influence on the environment. For long, global discourse struggled to keep the consequences of this destructive influence out of sight, out of mind.

In *Tastes of Nature*, Cameroonian poet, playwright, and environmentalist Ekpe Inyang seeks to break this monologue of globalization and, once more, let the dialogue between Nature and Culture take the stage. This is not done naïvely, by pretending that modernity never took place. In these poems, we never find the belief in a simple return to innocence, nor a nostalgic yearning for a paradise before the Fall. On the contrary, Inyang stays grounded in conservational practices, in the daily interaction with his environment, and the findings of scientific research. His primary aim is to show how local places and global spaces are interconnected through ecological systems, and this ambition stems from a cheerful and sincere admiration for the lush beauty of the natural world.

We find in these poems a deep-felt awareness of the inadequacy of global discourse. "Yet Another Debate" provides us with a striking image of the frustrating inability of the global elite to take care of global concerns. What is the point of yet another climate conference which simply reproduces the problems it puts to discussion? For, what we experience today is how global warming, somewhat paradoxically, marks the end of globalization, as it becomes clear how globalized economics never was able to fully repress the physical world. The ghost of materiality comes back to haunt us in the form of acid rain, rising temperatures, and species extinction. Even a world without borders has its limits and thresholds. Consequently, the poet urges us to stop flying all over the world, going from one conference to another, engaging in endless, fruitless discussions, "wasting foods, drinks and funds/ that would have fed millions of the poor". Instead, it is time we, as Inyang puts it in another poem, started to "understand the nature of nature".

To achieve that understanding, we need to leave the *global* perspective to take on a *planetary* view on the world – that is, a world interconnected not only by networks of exchange but also by natural forces, ecological systems, and biological communities. It is fitting, then, that *Tastes of Nature* starts in space, or, at least, with acknowledging how we earthlings are already in it. Just like each one of us is engaged in local and global environments, we are also part of a cosmic ecology. Ecology has no outer limit. In the opening poem, "Our New Home?", the poet is curiously prying an alien planet in the sky, pondering the amusing yet terrifying thought whether, perhaps, this may become our new home in the universe. Whereas the idea of Mars colonization has been a common trope in speculative science fiction for ages, today, and due to the immediate threats of global warming, this is also a very real concern guiding the efforts of numbers of actual scientists, philosophers, and entrepreneurs. As Earth becomes uninhabitable, perhaps we – or a select few of us – must leave Earth behind, making a new home in the cosmos.

Inyang visualizes interplanetary migration in erotic terms. The new world is a bride, "ripe and ready" to be wooed into marriage. Through this use of metaphor, the poet suggests how the language of space colonization simply reinvents the colonialist, imperialist trope of the virgin land: space is up for grabs, ready for the taking. There is a certain amount of ambiguity to be found in the poet's praise for the "stubborn intelligence" of modern scientists, whose "sophisticated flying machines" have scouted this new Dark Continent, taking almost pornographic pictures "from length to breadth, sizing you up". Speaking of space colonization, we tend to repeat the ideology of manifest destiny and reckless exploitation, which, to be honest, brought us into this dire situation, in the first place. It seems appropriate that the opening poem is charged with both excitement and caution, as the very same words may be read as both a critique of and a tribute to the exceptional feats of humanity.

What is interesting is how this grand apotheosis of scientific progress is precisely what brings us down to the level of animals, insects, even the probing roots of the great Iroko tree, as it shows how we all rely on the space surrounding us for support. Like every other species, humans must carve out their niche from very specific environmental conditions, and when these conditions change, we are forced to explore and adapt. In this new collection of Inyang's poetry, it is impossible not to read the opening poem in relation to the moral fable of "The Bees" (originally published in *Silent Voices*, 2011). In that poem, we find a group of bees in search of a new home, that is, "hollow trees to make their hives". (Perhaps, our Mars is their "tree that could contain/ No less than a million and one/ Hives"!) In the bee poem, the global elite – the Queens and Drones – employ new destructive technologies in the form of lethal spider webs, with little concern for the harm they cause to the workers who provide them with sustenance. Finally, the elite is driven away, and while searching for a vacant spot of their own, they end up in the spider's web. Is this not a cautionary tale, reminding us of SpaceX and Blue Origin, that is, private, commercial initiatives to colonialize space, already in progress today?

But why all this talk about space? Isn't eco-poetry supposed to be about flowers and forests, rivers and mountains? They certainly have their prominent place, too, in Inyang's poetry. There is no shortage of localized places and close environments, as the planetary perspective is never allowed to block the astonishing views of Fako, Muanenguba or the Bakossi Mountains. However, by opening his collection with the view on Mars, the poet reminds us of one of the most important insights of ecological thinking, namely, that no biotope is cut off from its surroundings. The homes in which we dwell are always larger than we imagine; it is not a question of where one ecological system ends and another begins, but in what ways one system connects to another.

According to modern ideology, waste simply disappears out of sight – dumping it in the ocean is like flushing your filth down the toilet. Inyang often returns to the topic of pollution, as in "River Ohompe", where the life-giving river is paid back for its services – providing the people with drinking water, fish, and clear baths – by having the very same people literally shitting right into its mouth. The poem underlines how waste prevails even when left out of sight; in the case of excrements, it comes back to haunt the people in the form of diarrhoea, typhoid and other bacterial infections. By poisoning the water, we poison ourselves; by shitting into the river, we shit into our mouths. Today, we must learn that even the things we do not see still exert a forceful impact on us and the systems that sustain us. And still, the simple fact that space is starting to fill up with all kinds of so-called space debris or space pollution – that is, defunct human-made objects left behind orbiting the Earth – shows how we simply have expanded the excremental ideology of waste from a local to a global, and finally, planetary scale. (It must be stressed, in this context, that the global waste trade primarily follows garbage produced in the Global North being disposed of in the Global South).

There is a further, more fundamental, cosmic dimension to Inyang's poetry. The poet is in love with the world: he is mesmerized by the splendour of life and the majestic landscapes that harbour it, and he often loses himself in pastoral reverie. But Inyang is also aware of the elemental forces that make life possible, in the first place. Most central in this regard is the sun as the energetic source of all earthly exuberance. In the almost delirious "Beautiful Sunshine", the poet seems drunk on love as the sun rays touch "the smooth dark skin of beauty". Heat is not enough, though; left on its own, the sun scorches the earth, and it needs the company of water for life to thrive. Thus, in "Plants Sing Songs" it is not the shining light but the darkening face of the rainstorm that makes the plants sprout "in their numbers/ to sing/ songs of praise".

In "Rain and Sun", Inyang playfully depicts the dynamics between elemental forces in terms of two contenders exchanging blows in a grand game of boxing. Such an extensive use of personification reminds us of the great pantheons of world mythologies, where the often-petty squabbles of gods impact the lives of humans. Myths are relevant today, for in mythical thinking we find an expression of the very thing sought after by contemporary scientists and philosophers, namely, a way of imagining and representing the agencies of the natural world. In myth, as in poetic personification, we see nature as something more than a mechanical system of dead lumps of matter. The mythic worlds are pervaded by wills, wants, and whims of their own. Is this not what our complex ecological models are grappling with, in their own way? Poetry and ecological research have a lot to learn from each other.

If the sun is the source of all living energies – of plants, animals, and humans alike – life itself relies on a cosmic ecology. Sun and rain provide without ever wanting anything in return. As it is stated in the poem with that name, "Rain" expresses "unreserved love to brethren". Yet, the striking image of the sun and the rain as ferocious fighters also displays their violent tendencies. When the sun gives too much of himself, we have draught; and with the unrestrained charity of the rain follows surges and floods. Latent in the image of the boxers, then, is an understanding of the fragile balance between us and the tremendous forces on which we depend.

"The Sun" depicts the solar power as a fierce and boisterous lover, shooting out "a million tongues" to smother the earth in kisses. In this poem, the sun's love comes across as a duplicitous force, not unlike the Greek *pharmakon*: both a remedy and a poison. The sun gives life; yet, left without measure, its healing powers turn lethal. In love, there is always the risk of devouring the other. Passion needs to be balanced with protection.

Inyang often returns to the image of the ozone layer as the great "umbrella of life", sheltering Mother Earth from the raging "bonfire in space", as he puts it in one of his poems about global warming, "Life-threatening Fever". With the depletion of the ozone layer, the stratosphere becomes unable to absorb the ultraviolet radiation of the sun. Instead, an excess of heat becomes trapped under the "thick blanket" of carbon dioxide pollution, leading to an enhanced greenhouse effect. In the poem "Ozone", Inyang thus demonstrates how metaphor and mythic personification, far from being frivolous or even primitive means of communication, is fully compatible with a scientific explanation, as the image of the umbrella transforms into a weirdly poetic description of how "aerosols hiding in/ Chlorofluorocarbons whose single chlorine atom when released/ Destroys thousands of your molecules in one catalytic reaction".

When reading Inyang it is important to understand the role of the poet as a teacher. In *Tastes of Nature*, we certainly find a decent amount of Theocritean *idyll*, that is, brief scenes from everyday life, with the poet in intimate connection to his bucolic surroundings. "Mud Wasp" is a beautiful example of this. But equally prevalent is the didactic tone of Virgilian *Georgics*, painting the bigger picture of the struggles between mankind and the natural world. Inyang even shares with Virgil a particular fondness for comparing humans to bees! Be more like the bee and less like the fly, the poet encourages us in "Like the Soil". This means, bypass the pile of crap and search for nectar among the flowers. Or, better yet: "be like the silent soil", who turns excrements into beautiful crops that feed the many.

There is simplicity in Inyang's poetry, a clarity stemming from the will to communicate; the poet means what he says, and he says it for a reason. There is no place for mystification nor obfuscation. Like any good teacher, he spends less time wagging his finger at us, than using it to point out various points of interest in his surroundings, thus sharpening the ecological awareness of his readers. He details the significance of particular species and relates their place in the great scheme of things.

In the catalogue of creatures taking up the second part of the current collection, Inyang dispels the irrational fears and prejudices we project onto certain animals, teaching us, instead, about the ecological services they provide. Whereas "The Owl" of the poem of that title has traditionally been associated with witchcraft, the poet makes an effort to explain what ecosystem services the bird provides. The poem ends with the poet declaring his gratitude to the animal who used to scare him as a child. This is a *Bildungsroman* in miniature, a story about ecological education, itself turned into a didactic poem.

In a poem about bats, much like the philosopher Thomas Nagel in his classic paper "What Is It Like to Be a Bat?", the poet expresses his inability to fully understand the bat's strange phenomenology of echolocation. And nevertheless, he is still able to realize its ecological function as someone who helps to spread the seeds of fruit trees over vast distances. Difference does not stand in the way of appreciation. In "The Elephant", the poet even refers explicitly to scientific studies to dispel certain prejudices against the animal. Whereas the crop-raiding behaviour of elephants may bring them into conflict with large-scale farming, their tendency to push down trees also "Opens up the canopy for sunlight to hit/ The forest floor, giving life to dormant seeds". In so doing, the large and unruly creature ensures the health of the forests. And humans, too, – yes, even farmers! – rely on the forests' capacity to transform carbon dioxide into oxygen.

Most importantly, *Tastes of Nature* is a project of celebration. First of all, the poems collected here ask us to slow down for a second and absorb our lush surroundings. Look, listen, and savour the rich flavours of the world! Inyang acknowledges the severity of the present situation, but he never gives in to despair. Throughout these poems, we find an almost stubborn refusal to give up on hope. In its final stage, the poems present an imperative for action – a determined call to "Join the fight to change climate change". Perhaps, I am a bit more cynical than the poet, since I find little solace in the promise of clean and green technologies that "still make huge profits", as he puts it in "Who Says We Can't". But let's hope, for the sake of all of us, that Ekpe is right.

Erik van Ooijen
Author of *Nattens ekologi: Naturen, kulturen och den mÖrka vänd-ningen* (*Ecology of Night: Nature, Culture and the Dark Turn*)
Associate Professor of Comparative Literature, Mälardalen
University, Sweden

Part One
Nature's Wonders

There is more in and about Nature than we currently know and may ever know, but the little we know is sufficient to lay the bricks for the foundation to inform our choices and decisions.

Our New Home?

I see you in orbit, so beautiful
not too far from Earth where I live
but yet lifeless, I hear

I hear on you have
recently been landing
sophisticated flying machines

made by some of us with stubborn
intelligence, to take pictures of you
from length to breadth, sizing you up

as if to woo you into marriage
and to ask if you are ripe and ready
to accommodate humankind

Now let me ask you boldly
as I stand here watching you
curiously from Earth

and you answer me as it's asked
without fear or favour
are you ready to be our new home?

9 November 2019

Wonders of Nature

at day overhead
sun shines
so bright
giving out
heat waves

wakes in dazzling
colour of silver
sleeps in
that of glittering gold
but slowly giving way to

moon and stars which
in the dead of night
shine so bright
but dishing out
air so cool and lulling

caressing drowsy jaws
churning out silver notes
like snowflakes flying in the air and
gathering to produce melodies of gold
that create wonders of nature

23 January 2021

Asteroids

At first, it was such a great spectacle,
with daily reports on radio, television
and the social media, reports
generating both curiosity and silent fear.

Great minds have been seeing you tumbling down
in space, but now one of you - so big –
was quite close to earth, after billions of years
in its endless journey steadily on its orbit.

In a universe that keeps on expanding
turning and stretching itself always into infinity
your journey in search of a landing
becomes even more indeterminate.

I hear you're named asteroids, scattered
pieces of rock in space after that primordial blast -
the Big Bang! Some of you are larger than earth,
and you're now in near collision with earth?

I guess it was a most forbidden hug,
sending chills down the spines even
of great minds - top scientists - who know and say
just an inch of a shift from an orbit can cause a collision.

What would it mean to life – especially us - on earth?
What really caused your derailment from orbit,
violating the law of physics? Thank goodness,
those great minds guided you back and away onto orbit

in time to avert another apocalypse, just in time
to prevent the imminent celestial war, the type
known to have blasted earth, millennia

ago, into its current form, content and place.

9 November 2019

Sonnet of Nature Walk

(First published in *Eni and Other Poems*)

It was scorching
But I set off for a walk
Stubborn as I am
Through a glade so scary
Picking a path snaky
Exuding sweat real sticky
Panting like a dog utterly thirsty
Trudging like a cockroach long, long sick
Then came the breeze gusty
And I felt so refreshed
The air now sweetly scented
Flowers on both sides brightly coloured
Waving in patterns mesmerizing
Ushering me to the kingdom of floral beauty

12 March 2015

Reading the Stars

(First published in *Just a Bend*)

The moon is in its full form
Sits she in the dark starry sky
I look up and see the stars
Forming letters that a story tell
A great story it must be
A story that points the way
The easy way to everything
But I'm so illiterate in the signs
And need someone greater
Wise enough to read the stars for me

7 July 2019

In the Blue Sky

(First appeared in *Caught Between,* unpublished)

I look across
the massive blue,
observing the rise and fall
of rolling,
wavy sheets,
missed
sharks and whales
in predatory acrobatic displays
greeted with ululations
and thunderous applauses
that sound so distant,
but
hit the fine line of the horizon
in the far, far reaches,
where
the sun
daily rises
on steely wings of
light blue and bright purple
and sleeps
on a giant bed of rose and gold
laced with colours
of
the rainbow
boldly cutting
across
the vastness
of the moist, blue sky
now studded
with soaring eagles,
parrots, and sparrows,
a new brand of stars

dancing to one of nature's
sweet, healing melodies.

14 August 2019

The Waves

(First appeared in *No Stress*, unpublished)

I was sitting on a rock
Somewhere near a dock
Listening to the waves
Spreading out their dunes

I was sitting on a hill
Housing a hornbill
Listening to the waves
Yarning 'way their tunes

I was sitting in my room
Now in hand a broom
Watching at the waves
Dancing to their tunes

I was sitting in my bed
Outside sky now red
Watching at the waves
Folding 'way their dunes

10 May 2017

Blue Sky

(First published in *Just a Bend*)

Let them yell
Like big bell
Let them cry
Like dragonfly
Let us love
Like humble dove
Let's unite
And let's ignite
Making the eye
So, so bright
So, so bright
Like the blue sky

1 June 2019

Early in the Morning

(For Joy Eni Inyang and her friends all over the world)

It's so early
in the morning,
the sky
is blinking,
the wind
is blowing,
the birds
are singing
their songs;
the frogs
are dancing,
the trees
are clapping,
and people
listening
from beds.

24 June 2020

Rain

(First appeared in *No Stress*, unpublished)

She sent down her long wetting arms
Released herself to mingle with men
Embraced huge crowds with such charm
Expressing unreserved love to brethren
But received such disgusting hate
Like from a lady not ready for a date

7 July 2018

Soft Breeze

(First published in *Just a Bend*)

Feel the softness of the breeze
that rushes in
listen to the music
between the leaves
open your heart and let the music
steal away your worries and your fears
open it widely and let it drop in
the sweet parcel it bears for you

16 June 2019

Thieving Rain

(First published in *Dangerous Pastime*)

Friday
It touched the ground
Pounding
Left the land flooding
Pushed the Sun to the front
Slept behind snoring
Refusing
It ever came out of its bed
That day

27 June 2014

Rain and Sun

(First published in *Just a Bend*)

Sun was first
to hit
the ring
taking full sway
pacing
up and down
taunting
contender
up until mid-day
beating the floor
boastfully
with his harsh
ray-feet
to prove he's
still in charge
to proclaim
he's the title
holder even
in this season
when most
spectators don't speak
much of him.
Then comes
the contender
the most
heralded contender
Rain
panting
ranting
sweating
beating his chest
boasting

he'll fling
Sun
out of the ring
like a piece of paper
frightening
and
causing crowds
of spectators
to run
for shelter
from his
known drenching
and piercing blows
in such times
of expressed fury.
Referee Thunder
obviously
biased towards
Rain
suddenly
blows the whistle
after
his assistant
Lightning
has split the dark sky
with the
flashy blinks of
his electrocuting eyes
as signal
and the fight
begins
causing
Rain to sweat
even more
profusely
knowing he faces
the title holder
after all
as Sun

is still beating
the floor of the ring
in cruel contempt
even as Thunder
now starts
to rumble wildly
in readiness to shoot
sharp blue blows
in overt
angry support
to increase the sweat
of contending
Rain
and flood
the floor
to cause
Sun
to slide and fall
and fly away
back up
in the dark, dark reaches
above the sky.

31 August 2019

The Sun

(First appeared in *Caught Between,* unpublished)

Do you see the Sun
shooting out
a million tongues?

Tongues to kiss
the earth
and all on it depend.

Tongues radiating
energy that powers
earth and life.

Tongues emitting it
in small measures so
it does not instead

the earth consume.
Everything measured
so kissing doesn't become

lethal, so loving is not fatal
so life is not consumed
by the energy of love, so

the Sun continues
radiating only energy
that heals the earth.

11 August 2019

The Moonlit Night

(First published in *Silent Voices*)

Three moons had slipped past
Yet children slept at dusk
At dusk came darkness thick
A thing the kids abhorred

Occupied was every mind
In supplication for her smile
For her face to light the land
And fill each heart with bliss

Then came one quiet evening
As the clouds drifted by
Came happy shouts of children
Jumping from house to house

Parents the message could guess
The golden face had shown
Knew they what else would follow
To mark the glamourous night

Gathered at Village Square
Children in their numbers
One great circle they formed
Like the face in the sky

Sang they songs of war and peace
Songs of toil and joy
Of death and birth
Songs composed by great poets

Beautiful Sunshine

(First published in *Eni and Other Poems*)

Beautiful, beautiful, beautiful, beautiful
When at last Day raises her curtain
To display but soft, soothing sunshine
Beautiful, beautiful, beautiful, indeed

Beautiful, beautiful, beautiful, beautiful
In the baking-hot seaside city of Limbe
Where Fako's skirt soaks in Atlantic
Beautiful, beautiful, beautiful, indeed

Beautiful, beautiful, beautiful, beautiful
On the Atlantic Coast of Cameroon
Sun now soothes the smooth dark skin of beauty
Beautiful, beautiful, beautiful, indeed

27 April 2016

At the Beach

Unbelievable how quickly I got there.
I was walking in a contemplative mood.
What was I really thinking about?
It was my first experience as a baby,
when I was taken to that beach.

Then I thought it took ages
just to get there.
Dad and Mom walked me there.
They made me walk such a great distance.
In silent tears I did. I didn't know why

they made me walk instead of carrying me.
Why did I have to go through all that?
But once Mom told me I must grow
into a strong man like Dad, and added,
"It's just a short distance and soon we'll be there."

Tears dried up fast. Immersed in a sea of splendour!
Clear blue water in soft, gentle waves.
Pure white sand in the astonishing vastness.
Pebbles like diamonds arranged in distinct teams.
Boulders of amazing shapes standing in inviting postures.

I must have covered seven times
the distance I cried to walk there
running from one fascinating display
to another. Mom and Dad, too, were
savouring the gallery, taking in the cool breeze,

Over there, like I can touch it with my hands,
I now see so clearly where the sky
meets the sea, where the Sun rises and sets,

where the rainbow rises to cut across the sky,
where Nature displays her magnificent beauty.

13 November 2019

Part Two
In Praise of Species

The importance of wild species, the roles they play, the services they render, and the intricate interactions and dependencies amongst them are useful sources of experiences that can shape our worldviews and guide our actions and reactions.

The Owl

You look so great
yet so frightful,
with eyes as beautiful

as ours and as sharp
as the eagle's, though
with claws less frightful.

Your neck you can turn almost
three hundred and sixty degrees,
to see all around and about you.

Your feathers are soft and light
like cotton from the wild cotton tree
at our village school, and your flight

is so graceful and silent. And
you so easily fetch your prey
spotted from atop that tall tree.

Your nightly hooting makes us think
you are the originator
or key promoter of witchcraft.

But you are there doing
a great service to us.
Just like the snake, you swallow up

rats that would have invaded
our homes in large numbers.
I can tell this from the pellets you spit

down on the foot of that tree
where you roost and send out

your nightly hooting near our homes.

As a child, I feared you and also
associated you with witchcraft, but now
I've learnt about you, and I thank you.

9 November 2019

Beware Quick Conclusions

(First published in *Eni and Other Poems*)

The dog barks in front of the house
The fox sneezes near the pigsty behind
The lizard nods its head on the wall in the living room
Guess, what's going on?

The cock crows atop the house roof
The guinea fowl cackles in the bush
The lizard nods its head on the wall in the living room
Guess, what's going on?

The pussy cat meows under the table
The lion roars in its den in the wild
The lizard nods its head on the wall in the living room
What next is your conclusion?

15 April 2016

The Bees

(First published in *Silent Voices*)

A group of bees set out to search
For hollow trees to make their hives
This was in a distant country
Where nobody had ever been

They found a tree that could contain
No less than a million and one
Hives that could each contain no less
Than a million above the Queens

And all around the tree they found
Flowers beautiful like the Sun
Flowers that contained what they need
Nectar for their honey-factory

Day by day some bees were busy
Building hives to house their great Queens
Collecting nectar and pollens
To feed the Queens and Drones and all

Honour had the Drones to mate with
Queens that had to lay all the eggs
While workers spent their time to work
To feed the Queens and Drones and all

The workers worked without complaint
They worked with joy and love and zeal
But came a time when Queens and Drones
Employed some Spiders to build webs

So busy were the workers that
They took no notice of the webs

And each day ten or more did fall
And got entangled in a web

On the whole, there were a hundred webs
Hundred webs against million hives
Workers were then so threatened that
They drove the Queens and Drones away

The Queens and Drones went on and on
Searching for vacant hollow trees
Their search brought them back where they came
And got entangled in a web

Bat and Cave

When I hear
the word cave,
I think of you.

But even out of the cave you form a huge sack
hanging from tall trees
as you in your numbers

huddle and cuddle,
occasionally flying about
so, so swiftly in great numbers

without one hitting the other,
something I can't explain
why in such speed it never happens.

You hang head-down,
and I wonder whether
that's to make your

blood flow more into
your head to
nourish your brain with oxygen,

and strengthen your sense
of echolocation as you oft make
long trips for fruits on yonder trees.

They say in the day you see not, and I
wonder why at night you do so
perfectly, doing such acrobatic feats.

You puzzle me whether you are
mammal or bird, with such great wings,

like umbrella or parachute,

taking you so fast in flights,
from one fruit tree to another,
and you help us spread the seeds

far and near, like the elephant
and other mammals and
and birds like parrots and hornbills,

keeping our forests rich and healthy,
to provide us with services, from fruits
and fibres, air and water to leisure.

9 November 2019

The Peacock

Brightly coloured
Brave and proud
Large tail feathers
Spread out like
Rare regalia of
An Indian queen
Mistaken for pride
Shaped like heart
It's a spread of love

11 January 2020

Strange Creatures

(First published in *Just a Bend*)

the hooting owl
with a visage like your own
you quickly searched for words
and rebranded
witch-bird that brings you misfortune

the crawling snake
with a shape like a monkey's tail
if not like a worm
that in your stomach dwells
you name serpent 'cos some do bite

these 'strange creatures'
that you treat with so much hate
may be the reason you've lost a trillion
rats with which you once shared house
that stole your food and ate your shoes and feet

16 June 2019

Chameleon

Chameleon, I greet thee
Sometimes looking red
Sometimes looking green

Chameleon, I salute thee
Sometimes really black
Sometimes really white

Chameleon, I hail thee
Sometimes appearing so sick
Sometimes appearing so well

Chameleon, I dove my hat for thee
Sometimes proving so fragile
Sometimes proving so strong

30 August 2020

It's Christmas Time

mountains
still stand
so tall
lie valleys
in deep silence

rivers, streams
less swift-flowing
moons and stars
seeming low
like they can
our heads touch

sky's blueness
rather greying
forests' green
yellow, brown, red
cold silent bites
in whistling breeze

birds' melodies
now much sweeter
as the air is filled
with scents sweeter
than perfumes dear
which gives the message

loud and clear
so loud and clear
warming our hearts
the message that
Christmas is near

23 December 2019

Do You See?

(First appeared in *Caught Between*, unpublished)

Do you see
What I see?
Do you smell
What I smell?

I see
    loads
        of bees

Swarming
The flower plant.
I smell the sweet smell
Of honey sweet.

11 August 2019

Song of a Baby

(First published in *Dangerous Pastime*)

Tell the lion Lie on
And the python Pry on
Say to the chicken Chip in
But not to weevil Wee ill

16 March 2014

My Honey Source

(First appeared in *No Stress,* unpublished)

From you, I get sure honey
Though sometimes after a sting
Honey that gives me money
Now my hives no humming

Children need that honey-sweet
Even parents also need
Can I send you a quick tweet?
Your help is needed indeed

Surely your nectar source's gone
As men set axes on trees
More hives I have paid for done
Men, please come pay back the fees

26 April 2017

Crickets

(First appeared in Caught Between, unpublished)

Cranky,
crooked
crickets daily rise from their
commodious,
capacious,
cavernous
caves,
clinging to the
carcinogenic
crowns,
citadels of greatness,
craning their necks,
croaking and
crowing but apparently
crawling and
crushing under loads of more
cunning
crooks
craving for more to the self, thus
contravening the
canons of
common property use.

15 August 2019

The Elephant

(First published in *Just a Bend*)

Have you ever seen the elephant live?
I know you've seen it more in pictures,
Moving and still; so interesting, isn't it?
Charismatic, keystone, flagship species!
Seen the trunk? Very like a big snake!
Indeed, a prehensile hand!
And the ears? Like huge ceiling fan blades!
Seen its tail to whisk off tsetse flies?
And huge tusks attractive to poachers?

There exist two types of elephants –
Savannah elephant, forest elephant,
The savannah type is a little bigger.
Elephant, elephant, elephant, elephant,
Biggest terrestrial animals in size
But not in population ever-dwindling
Due to poaching and habitat shrinkage
From rising deforestation more for timber
But also for roads and huge plantations
Driving herds to farms and plantations,
Bringing these in conflict with us
As they display their crop-raiding behaviour.

Know anything good about the elephant?
Research findings by Dr James Powell
And other top researchers on the mammal:
Seeds of more than fifty species of plant
Germinate only after passing through
It's guts that serve as treatment chambers
In the laboratory of life and sustainability.
That it forages on such a wide variety
And in such great bulk also means

Its huge guts-wastes surely enrich
The thin forest soils and serve as mediums
For species to disperse and sprout to life
In areas that never once saw them,
The elephant enjoys such a huge home range.

Its behaviour of pushing down trees
Opens up the canopy for sunlight to hit
The forest floor, giving life to dormant seeds,
Causing shade-suppressed species
To pick up and swim towards their fullness,
Ensuring the very health of our forests
That consume tons of carbon dioxide
To stabilize our climate changing.

9 July 2019

The Spider

Who learnt from the other:
You from Grand Dad
or Grand Dad from you?

I used to admire
how Grand Dad wove it.
Taking the thread in and out.

But you do it differently.
Seems like the thread
is buried in your tummy,

as I see a line running out
through your anus.
My grand Dad buys his from

the market and rolls it
round a spool. But yours
I can't see where it's rolled,

except the line that runs out
of your anus as you move about
to do the work. Can I really

call yours weaving? Your skill and
tools and thread are simply magic.
And you produce something

better than Grand Dad's net
which Dad uses for fishing.
Even better than Dad's singlet

that I once wore to take a photo
with Dad, Mom, my younger brother

and my aunty that loves us.

My Grand Dad's for fishing.
And yours is for...? Oh, I see!
A fly and a mosquito caught in your net.

12 November 2019

Gorilla

Gorilla, I see you with my clear eyes
Muscular, bulky, gigantic
Living purely on plants
Though looking
Like one devouring massive flesh

As an ape, on knuckles, you walk
Searching for food and water
In the forest rich in plants of all sorts
Hitting your chest heavily
Once in a while, as you run

Soon you'll become
A silverback
Wanting no other male around
But keeping all the females to yourself,
As a sign you are the greatest

Your chest you hit so hard
Once in a while, as you run briefly
Creating such a spectacle but
Also announcing and demonstrating
Determination of your territory to protect

4 November 2019

Mud Wasp

It was your shrilly, whistling sound
that diverted my attention that morning,
and I saw you live in full action.

I was still lying in bed, reflecting
on a critical conservation challenge,
but you drew my full attention.

I followed you at that rare display of
Creativity for hours on hours on hours;
you maintained the same rhythm,

working to build that exquisite edifice
from scratch, before my own eyes;
and I couldn't believe what I saw.

From a little spray of very soft mud
you simply used to stain a spot
on the wall, you carried on adding more,

doing what I couldn't really describe,
except imagining you were dancing
with your head, whistling that thrilling song.

Spellbound was I that from that tiny stain on the wall
there was that great transformation; but, unfortunately,
I didn't count how many trips you made for the mud.

I took late breakfast that day, for all
I could remember, as you gripped
my attention so tenaciously I could not

wake, more for fear I might interrupt you

in that mind-blowing architectural project...
from that little stain on the wall to that full house!

11 November 2019

Giant Scissors

Looking at that inspiring picture,
Framed on a sky-blue background,
In which his hands are stretched
Upwards – skywards – and feet
Stretched out wide, sideways, so
Determinedly firm on the ground,
Anchored like the roots of Iroko tree
Deep down in the soil of life's web,
In that fascinating position to keep fit
And stay always and forever alive,
And having observed him
In his distant past and recent activities,
Some so good and some so bad,
I now know and can safely say
Man's but a giant pair of scissors
Used to trim the rough edges of life's
Fine linen of collective endeavours,
But which is often used to
Brutally tear the mighty fabric apart,
For reassembly in pots. Plates. Cups...
A million vessels of pride and pleasure.

19 July 2020

Part Three
The Dialogue Begins

The incessant dialogue between Culture and Nature highlights the difficulty in negotiating common ground, and in the end, the one shapes the other, with the weak and fragile likely to be placed under stress.

Nature and Culture

Nature
and Culture
once lived with great pleasure

engaged in such great dialogue
producing such a great catalogue
to break the stage of monologue

When Nature stands up singing
Culture starts dancing, ringing

her bells of support in rare gratitude
as a conscious change in attitude

so Nature and Culture should ever
remain in great harmony forever

9 November 2020

Listening to Iroko

I sit here
on this hard rock of life
admiring the ever-dancing waves

I sit here listening to the great
Iroko tree across the lake
that's given tongues to her parts

I sit here listening
listening in rapt attention
listening like never before

I can hear
the shooting of her flowers bursting
to peep the brightness of the Sun

I can hear
the whispering of her leaves
in the rushing wind and washing rain

I can hear
the stretching
of her trunk in determined growth

I can hear
the cracking
of her roots running underneath

roots on errands deep down
in the great magnitude
of soil's silent depth

I can hear
everything the tree is saying

through the tongues of her parts

I can hear every word
word of scarcity, pain and despair
word of abundance, joy and hope

I can hear, I can hear
I can hear every single word
I can hear

19 August 2020

Silent Voices

(First published in *Silent Voices*)

Lions roar
Dogs bark
Pigs whine
When danger they sense

And decide to announce
Their knowledge of it
And scare and caution
The serpent in action

Pangolins roll themselves into balls
Porcupines spread out their piercing quills
When danger they sense
And decide to act in self-defence

But Giant Rats retreat into their tunnels
And Snails simply withdraw
Into their dry shells
And decide to speak in silent voices

Silent voices
Are a warning sound
Of impending doom,
The lightning that goes
Before the crack of thunder

The Tree

(First published in *Death of Hardship*)

I
Hear
You sulking
Day and night,
Complaining
About the biting, freezing cold,
About the burning heat, about hunger and
Starvation, you who have legs to run and hands with which
To till and build. Were it that you were me, embracing the raw
Cold
And
Heat
And
Mad
Storms
And floods,
Sensing the
Seasons come
And go, 200
Rounds,
January to
December,
Dancing on the
Same spot under
The naked sky, giving
Shelter, receiving none,
What story would you tell?

1 July 2011

The New Song (1)

(First published in *Just a Bend*)

I've been listening to
The drops all through the night
Even deep in my sleep
I could hear them
Chanting the new song

I've been familiar with those
Drops ever since I was born
Right from my childhood
I've heard them
Chanting the new song

On my travels to distant lands
Those drops never ceased
Defining every path and step I took
As I continued to hear them
Chanting the new song

Let's drop the old tunes
Has been the message of the drops
Drumming on our consciousness
As they continue
Chanting the new song

On our roofs, on the streets
Same message
Drumming on our consciences
As the drops continue
Chanting the new song

8 June 2019

The plant

(First published in *Just a Bend*)

Birds and insects
Pay regular homage
To her for the flowers
That house sugary wells

Browsers always
There for the leaves
Monkeys transmuting
Via interlocking boughs

Feasting mostly on fruits
Some falling on the forest floor
For ungulates that may
Also go for the bark of the stem

Anchored by roots growing
Deep into the soil away from
Predation, avoiding instant
Withering of the plant

20 February 2019

Bakossi Landscape

(First published in *Silent Voices*)

There sit you wonderfully dressed
On the stool of Nature's splendour.
Possess you abundantly clearly
Unrivalled gifts of Mother Earth.
Thus gain you the title of Cameroon-microcosm,
The best-known AIM (Africa-In-Miniature),
In terms mostly of biodiversity.

Trees, tall, thick and green sway
Incessantly in the evening soothing breeze,
Restraining mad storms destruction-bound,
Skirting and capping and thus protecting Kupe
And Bakossi Mounts from harsh rays from the noon sky,
Holding and releasing in trickles pure sweat of life
That our thirst quench in the scourging heat of the day.

Grasses, tall and evergreen,
With dotted stunted trees,
Cover Muanenguba's bounteous breasts,
Nourishing twin Nature-wells atop her clear bald head.
Like giant eyes stare at the wells unblinking,
Keeping a keen watch over your entire outline
And distributing freshness for your untainted beauty.

In the lush and bloom of sundry flora,
Fauna, big and small, on you like lice sprawl,
Creatures that floral growth daily uphold,
And thus their abodes they maintain,
Guaranteeing these are with food littered,
Like pollen dust, hence ensuring,
In all certainty, their survival and ours.
Bakossi Landscape,

You truly really are
The pride of Cameroon,
The indelible emblem of Africa,
The jutting living legacy of Mother Earth,
The symbol of conservation,
The enviable heritage for posterity preserved.
The spirit
Of Culture
And Nature
You nurture,
And thus, you we must,
With undying ember of enthusiasm,
Serve to protect and project.

Renko

(First published in *Silent Voices*)

Renko the rock,
The pride of Korup,
The strength of a people long forgotten

Impressive glade you form
From canopy high
In the serene core of the jungle.

There you lie, a molten blanket
In magnificent splendour,
Like clear sky on forest floor

The glair, the lustre,
The glare, the glittering,
Like blinking of stars

In deep dark night.
The dazzling beauty
In the heat of the sun,

Hypnotising like the mystery tale
Reverberating past
Reminiscences of hunters

Who, having lost their bearings,
Roamed the jungle
And, wearily emerging

Unto your floor of benevolence,
Were served, as they sat, with
Assorted dishes from the blue

At the mention of "hunger".
Gone now the power is,
Shattered the benevolent heart as, we're told,

A hunter, greedy like a lion,
Broke all the plates in rage
After a heavy, sumptuous meal,

And now provide you can't
For hungry ones that miss their way,
And roam the Korup jungle,
And have the luck of meeting you.

Waterfall

(First published in *Death of Hardship*)

Waterfall.
Noisy.
Heard a thousand miles away.
Like a colony of weaverbirds
In the heat
Of a great assignment.
Digging even rocks
A thousand times faster
Than a thousand giant rats
Arranged in a fierce competition.
But not as deep as the less noisy ocean.

Waterfall.
Noisy.
Heard a thousand miles away.
Like a thousand caterpillars
On a great mission.
Clearing,
Digging,
Cracking,
Crushing,
Rolling rocks and debris.
But not as retentive as the less noisy ocean.

28 June 2011

Rock of Comfort

(First appeared in *Caught Between,* unpublished)

Now I take
respite in the serene space
away from the ceaseless
noises,
silly rantings
and vain gossips
on all sides,
and sit,
as usual,
savouring
the magical splendour
of the gently
rolling waves
of the lake yonder,
her magnificent beauty
engaged
in an endless embrace
with the light blue horizon
spewed with fine grains of gold.
She's so wonderfully
beautifully skirted
by a vast dark green
of nodding heads
and swaying, clapping boughs
that vanish gradually as
you run towards
the unseen silver lining of the horizon.
On that usual rock
padded with
blue and green
cushions of Nature's love,
laced with peace

and unmeasured kindness,
I sit,
listening to the rippling sound
of the rocky brook
running silently
meanderingly
underneath my tired feet,
exuding
exuberant
vibrations of astounding comfort,
soothing
my worried nerves
tensed by
that reawakening of
painful memories past.

15 August 2019

In the Ocean Depth

(First appeared in *Caught Between,* unpublished)

He finds myself
deep
in the ocean depth,
swimming
like
a whale,
hopefully not in a whale;
filled with the joy
of swimming in a body
so big,
carrying him
like a baby
in the softness of her arms
so warm,
taking him to places wondrous,
where
the sun soothingly
heats
his head
and where he can hardly see,
nor
feel anything
but hear
these
sweetly sounds
from beneath
and from above
and from all about him,
music reassuring,

telling him
he still carries the sac of life.

11 August 2019

Riches of Kenya

(First published in *Eni and Other Poems*)

The Great Rift Valley
Blinding beauty, rolling splendour
Making you giddy

Lake Naivasha
Teaming with terrestrial wildlife
Not beating aquatic lifeforms

Hell's Gate National Park
Nature's unrivalled architecture
Crafting scenes of unmatched standards
Site of international filmmaking

Nairobi National Park
Warehouse of wild wonders
Impala, zebra, giraffe, ostrich, crocodile, lion…

The Animal Orphanage
Inviting you to show your utmost care
Adding value to nature's gifts

15 May, 2016

Storm

(First published in *Death of Hardship*)

It started
Like a gentle breeze,
Caressing my cheeks.

Then, in a sudden burst,

It was a violent, whirly wind
Blowing down mansions of rock,
Tearing up giants of trees.

Just a moment.

Must I have, then, the highway crossed,
Erect like Iroko tree,
Walking, chest out, like Gorilla?

What wiser choice was there?

All around me I saw
Chimps, Buffalos, Elephants, Leopards,
Crocodiles, Giant Pangolins, Giant Lizards,

Even Gorillas, crawling like common lizards.

And on my knees, without delay,
I went,
Creeping like the beasts.

28 June 2011

Lamu

(For Zeinab, first appeared in *No Stress*, unpublished)

Love of pristine Nature
Artefact of fine Culture
Mother of great Civilisation
Umbrella of caring Humanity

18 February 2018

Part Four
Nature In Turmoil

Left alone, Nature has subtle ways of repairing itself, but with the over-whelming influence of human culture, it is always dressed in scars and fresh wounds that, in turn, expose humans to bitter experiences.

Flying Skirts

I see you more like a green belt
round Mother Earth
serving to hold her beautiful
skirts in place and in one piece

the skirts that dress Mother Earth and cover
all and sundry, from far and near,
from the harshness of furious skies
magic skirts that daily produce tons of oxygen

while sucking up more tons of carbon dioxide
that choke the atmosphere in that thick layer of
gases causing Mother Earth high fever

But now the skirts, being so attractive that
the belt is broken, is opened up for wholesale
full-scale plantations and logging or scrambling
for cash that leaves behind and spreads dust of sufferings

Look at the skirts flying in the winds
see them turbulently tossed up and down
hear them on earth roads choking in floods of tears
as, clearly, they're being stolen away…across the seas.

9 November 2019

Great Amazon

Great Amazon
viewed on the horizon

as I fly in the sky
returning from vacation on Skye

Magnificent greatness
in full expanse of neatness

intricately arranged by Nature
now weakened her duty to perform

From logging to poaching
and now to ravaging fires

the lungs of the earth
are systematically destroyed

9 November 2019

Imitation and Immigration

(First published in *Dangerous Pastime*)

Imitation
Has some limitation
Like immigration
Unlike emigration

Adaptation
Has some limitation
Like mitigation
Unlike mutation

Plantation
Has some limitation
Like deforestation
Unlike eutrophication

Production
Has some limitation
Like reproduction
Unlike repercussion

8 May 2014

Cry of the Woodpecker

(First published in *Silent Voices*)

so now you're out to set your axe
on one that makes my nest?
That's not fair, not fair at all,
i've hardly come to yours.
don't you know i too must survive
and have a place to live?
That's not fair, not fair at all,
i too need to live on.
look around, can you count them all,
how many you've annexed?
That's not fair, not fair at all,
you thought i don't need one?
and now even my only one
you want to rob me of?
That's not fair, not fair at all,
i too need to survive.
Now let's all make a sacred place
so we can live in peace;
danger may take us by surprise
if we don't think as one.

River Ohompe

(First published in *Silent Voices*)

Oh! River Ohompe
Your importance is so clear
You are our main source of water
For us to quench our thirst
The supplier of good fish as protein
For your poor, hungry children

In the hot tropical sun
You are our only saviour
We come to you for a cool, fresh bath
After a hard day's work
Oh, your importance is so clear!
So clear! So clear!

But we are ashamed to say
How everyday we pay you back
In funny, silly ways
We squat and shit right in your mouth
And throw dirt in your bed
Right in your bed!

We drain our toilets into you
We really poison you!
Ah! the recent Gamalin incident
That was certainly worse!
We killed the fish, both big and small
Gamalin won't spare one

Oh! River Ohompe
Your importance is so clear
But now something has gone wrong!
Something is certainly wrong!

No more fish to feed your children
No good water to quench their thirst

Diarrhoea, typhoid, come-no-go
So common these days! Mother
Ohompe, how we poison you
Everyday! Yes, poison you
And now receive our dose
Diarrhoea, Typhoid, come-no-go

The New Song (2)

(First appeared in *No Stress*, unpublished)

I took a walk to find flowers that smile
It must have taken me up to a mile
Listen everyone soon the bell will ring
Do you hear the song that the birds now sing?

Everyone sniffs around and get the smell
Don't look too much to instead get a spell
I did not know he's dumped such a huge pile
Which testifies he's got such a big bile

Yesterday I heard them sing the new song
Sung against the background of a huge gong
The message made me spellbound as I stood
And every meaning I then understood

23 April 2017

Like The Soil

(Inspired by Radhanath Swami's analogy of Bee and Fly, first published in *Just a Bend*)

Be like the searching bee
Bypassing
The rubbish mountains in you
And landing on
The flower deserts you have
In search of nectar,

Not like the hunting fly
Bypassing
The flower paradises in you
And landing on
The rubbish deserts you have
To feast on rotting particles;

Be like the silent soil
On whom every
Rubbish species we daily dump
But who, in return,
Blesses us with abundant crop,
Averting impending famine.

30 June 2019

The Tree Weeps

(First appeared in *Caught Between*, unpublished)

The tree weeps
as they hack
its trunk
with their cruel axes
and green tears
course down
its shivering leaves
as it starts
to sway
as a sign it's
about to touch
the hard ground
with obvious
possibility
of brushing
down shrubs
and herbs
that stoop
under it.

29 August 2019

Life-threatening Fever

(First published in *Silent Voices*)

i
Daily in pursuit
Of selfish development
Nations great enough
To play the steward of Mother Earth
Continue employing cheap
Technology to increase
Profit margins
For more affluence

Burning fuels
Containing gaseous grains
Carried by fumes thick and dark
Like tar
Up by winds to form
Above our heads

Thick blanket
Trapping heat to send back
To Mother Earth
Causing her to develop
Very high life-threatening fever

ii
Some gaseous grains
Escaping from our homes
Embark on a journey taking years
To wage a ruthless war with great Ozone

The umbrella of life over our Mother Earth
That prevents her and all that on her depend
From being consumed by raging

Flames of bonfire in space

By reducing them
To weak life-supporting rays
That now grow stronger and wild as
The umbrella above gets perforated
By the warring grains in space

Messily

(First published in *Eni and Other Poems*)

The day started drowsily
Waking us up noisily
Couldn't sit up easily
To get on busily
As it tumbled messily

9 August 2016

Worries and Cries

(First appeared in *Caught Between,* unpublished)

and
we are
systematically
immersed in
this rapidly
defrosting polar
of
more worries
about the weather,
more cries
about the climate,
already
experiencing more
erratic,
extreme,
devastating regimes
requiring
huge resources,
needing more innovations,
and
demanding greater
commitments to
bend the curve.

15 August 2019

Yet Another Whale

I heard it loud and clear
I saw the pictures
Gone viral
On Facebook
Shared
As proof
It happened
Again
Just yesterday
Yet another whale
Drifted to the shore
By senseless waves
Of the Atlantic
Found itself
Helpless
In their festive hands
Each dancing
With a knife
A machete
An axe
The life flesh
To harvest
In hungry
Celebration
Of that chance feast

They plunged into the rituals
Fell into full action
Deaf to cry for life
Listening not
To the painful wail
Of poor whale
Family numbers
Now fast plummeting

Known now to be
Critically endangered
As flesh-scooping
Nets, arrows and spears
Daily snatch their lives
Added to chance
Feasts on this coast
Of the Atlantic
In rhythmic
Hacking and song
That continue
Amidst massive
Spill of blood
That turn the massive waves
Into pure red
That embraces the golden glow
Of the setting sun
In perfect marriage

27 October 2019

Ozone

(First published in *Eni and Other Poems*)

Ozone
Produced within the tropics
Forming a thick layer over the far reaches of Mother Earth
High, high up in the stratosphere

Such a huge umbrella over Mother Earth
Protecting her and all lifeforms
Including humans of all civilizations
In North, in South, in East, in West from
Destruction by ultraviolet rays

Ozone
Such a friend when far, far away
But an abrasive enemy when close to Mother Earth
When your molecules are found in the troposphere

Your presence in the troposphere
Detected by humans with a good sense of smell
Or by rapid corrosion of earthly materials
Car tyres wearing faster than normal
Or some peculiar health problems

Ozone
Surely you also are destroyed as humans
Use fire extinguishers, refrigerators, aerosols hiding in
Chlorofluorocarbons whose single chlorine atom when released

Destroys thousands of your molecules in one catalytic reaction
Causing a hole in your protective stratospheric layer
Making Mother Earth and all lifeforms threatened

As a single stream of ultraviolet rays
May cause more than humans now estimate

18 April 2016

Changing Climes

(First published in *Just a Bend*)

The sky is choking
With incessant smoke from chimneys
Forests are
      Vanishing in lightning speed
Temperatures
Rising yearly
      Climes
Changing
Winds growing wild
      Roofs
Lifted off daily
Crops failing
      Hunger rising
Incomes
Plummeting
      Vulnerable communities
Rendered far more vulnerable
Death toll
      Soaring high

18 April 2018

We Have Been Messing the Air

(First appeared in *No Stress*, unpublished)

When the Wind sends down
Her turbulent waves
And Shrubs nod and bow in feigned abeyance
Some Tall Trees visibly waving goodbye
The Sun blinking and hiding her face in shame
The Sky shedding her long torrential tears
While women and children line up
Empty containers under roof-eaves
Only to realise Sky's longish tears
Now burn their heads on the slightest splash
And corrode the thirsty containers
On prolonged stay under the cascading eaves
Like furnaces melt certain metals
Engineered by skilled blacksmiths
To make bronze and steel and other harder metals
As all that now happens know the time has come
For general stock-taking how much
We have been messing the air
Year after year after year
And now can't flee from receiving
In such lethal form the mess we've been pumping up

1 June 2018

Plants Sing Songs

the sky
blinks
and lightning
runs to wipe
her darkening face
and thunder
blows his trumpet so loud
his thick
eardrums break
and rain
oozes out
sending down
her long wetting legs
to wear
the dusty trousers
of earth
and plants sprout
in their numbers
to sing
songs of praise
and man dances in
with huge baskets
for an endless harvest

9 January 2020

Fight Not to Be

(First published in *Dangerous Pastime*)

Cotton during harvest
Lead during planting

Cheetah at instructions
Snail at propping the tasks

Sheep in the dress
Wolf in the chest

Donkey in the eyes
Tortoise in the head

Pig in the party
Ant in the field

Bat in the day
Owl in the night

Cat in the pool
Dog in the manger

Dolphin in aqua-theatre
Shark in the sea

Dove on the table
Snake under the chair

Fight not to be
Scorpion that bites its tail

30 September 2014

Global Warming

(First published in *Eni and Other Poems*)

Carbon Dioxide?
Yes, my Lord, Carbon Dioxide is the lead actor
Ensuing from burning of fossil fuels
Running cars, lorries, generators, okadas and all
Not to mention industries and factories
With towering chimneys

Centres for producing products for our wants and needs
Even kitchens where cooking is done with biomass fuels
Daily to fill millions of stomachs
And come to think of diminishing forests
Whose trees would have been sucking up the excess in the atmo-
sphere
To reduce the thickness of the heat-trapping blanket

Water Vapour, Methane, Nitrous Oxide, and Ozone in the tropo-
sphere,
My Lord, appearing there in so much smaller quantities
Should not be brought under the same weight of international justice
Though collectively they form the blanket that envelops the earth
Trapping and sending heat that would have escaped into space
Back to warm the earth, again and again, causing global warming

19 April 2016

The Sun Flower

(First published in *Just a Bend*)

At sunrise, you show off your great beauty
Like carbide lamps of hunters on duty
Displayed exuberantly in the forest in fine rows
In the distance croaky sounds of crows
Pouring in perpetual nature's celebration
In the village dance steps in perfect calibration
At sundown, I hear this change in the tunes
Like hot deserts' rolling dunes
I lift my head to see those colours' brightness
Vanished, gone! All I now see is darkness
Turning happy celebrations into mourning
Phenomenon so far-fetched in the morning

22 June 2019

Nature of Nature

(First published in *Just a Bend*)

You fear to hear of acid rain
climate change, global warming
but fill the air with pollution

You don't wanna hear of species extinction
not even scarcity of plants and animals
but support logging, poaching and pollution

You hate to dream of earth without life
but keep destroying and polluting
plants, animals, that which is nature

Do you understand the nature of nature
the interconnectedness and interdependence
how it functions to support your life?

17 June 2019

Do You...?

Do you taste
your blood salty?
The acids sour?
The water tasteless?

Do you feel
Your heart ticking?
Your breath moving?
Your blood flowing?

Do you see
The seas rolling?
The mountains towering?
The rivers meandering?

Do you hear
the falls pounding?
The rain pouring?
The winds whistling?

Do you perceive
the cold biting?
The sun burning?
The air choking?

Do you note
humans making
machines drilling
technologies polluting?

Do you imagine
The state of Earth now?

A thousand years from now?
A million years from now?

28 December 2019

Nature

(First published in *Just a Bend*)

When storms grow wild
And tree boughs break
Leaves flying left and right
Dust forming a thick haze
Then bullet-like drops
Hit roofs so hard
You'll hardly hear
Any sound around
Save the mad aerial war
And your pounding heart
Nature can sometimes
Be so terrifying, like illness
To keep men as humble
As when they were born

20 February 2019

Soon into Dinosaurs

young and strong
like a great throng

smart and talented
yet so demented

turned into rhinosaurs
soon into dinosaurs

trust there are carnivores
where there are herbivores

30 December 2019

Part Five
Putting It Back Right

Our increasing understanding of the nature of Nature and the daily experiences of its tastes should motivate and drive us to seek sustainable ways of reversing its currently deteriorating state.

Yet Another Debate

Why are we here
coming from far, far away

flying long hours in the sky
in huge, huge numbers

flooding this city
ready for yet another debate

wasting foods, drinks and funds
that would have fed millions of the poor

polluting more the atmosphere
about which we are here to talk

to save the climate we keep hurting
when just enforcement of the law will do?

polluters must pay heavily
and brought to stop polluting thereafter

embrace they must green technologies
that must as secrets not be kept away

even from those not seen as ready
and technologically prepared

for the new race that is now run
only by the fastest on the lanes

if you don't want any more rats
in that house that you're now keeping

so clean and beautiful and attractive
help your neighbours to also clean theirs

9 November 2019

Debtors of Our Children

(Adapted from my published play, *The Hill Barbers*)

Understand you may not;
But a universal truth it remains
That debtors we have been
Right from that moment
When the first deep breath we took,
As acceptance of our sojourn
On this living ball of dust.

Debtors of our children,
Born and yet unborn;
Debtors of the future
Which from them we borrowed.

The debt today we enjoy,
Often so lavishly,
Wastefully and mindlessly,
Is borrowed capital,
The future
We've taken as a revolving loan
From our children,
Born and yet unborn.

To them the future belongs,
Our debt to them,
Which we all must pay back
In the self-same value
As we borrowed it, or higher.

Started, though, have we
The debt to pay.
By the care and tending
Our children already born we give.

But a tiny bit of the debt
That really is,
And the part remaining
Heavier and heavier on us grows,
As deeper and deeper
Into the capital we devour.

Sadness

There is sadness in my eyes
When I see green stretches
Turned into expanses of bare rock

There is sadness in my voice
When I hear people holding meetings
About mining the earth for more riches

There is sadness in my steps
When in solitude I walk kilometres
Without the green that flanked the path

There is sadness in my spirit
When I visit homes of Nature and hear
No creatures' sounds to welcome me

There is sadness in my soul
When I experience the heat and floods
Rising due to our senseless activities

There is sadness, sadness, sadness
Everywhere, even amongst the birds
That blessed new days with melodies

29 August 2020

Can Be Reversed

(First published in *Eni and Other Poems*)

Early and dearly in deepening thoughts
Sat I up in bed at dawn contemplating
Changes occurring too swift to comprehend
Inviting some disturbing moments
Loading a billion hearts with icy melancholy
Uncertainty colouring the sail of life
But I denounce that weird picture
In the unprecedented conviction that
Determined hope and verve can reverse
Events surely more malignant and catastrophic

1 July 2016

Big Opening

Just as you move in such fine dressings
So do I wish you even more blessings

Though our path has seen no crossing
Despite we partied with great tossing

I think it's time we got much closer
To share our skills so we're no loser

In a world where lots are happening
And I can see a really big opening

31 December 2019

Who Says We Can't?

(First published in *Just a Bend*)

Who says we can't stop
The spread of cancer,
Who says
Cancer can't be cured?

Who says we can't stop
The spread of HIV,
Who says
HIV-AIDS is incurable?

Who says we can't stop
Climate change,
Who says
Climate change is irreversible?

Who says we can't build clean
Technologies and still make huge profits,
Who says
Clean technologies are too expensive?

Who says we can't stop
The rising wars across the globe,
Who says
Wars are unstoppable?

If we can simply change the idle "can't"
To a big "can", negative thoughts to
Positive individual and collective actions,
Everything, indeed, is possible.

8 June 2019

How it Should Be

(First published in *Just a Bend*)

Let the breeze blow softly, softly
for trees
to nod their heads in the same rhythm
and birds to fly about with ease
as flowers show their brightly coloured heads
sweet scents opening our blocked nostrils
That's how it should be

Let the clouds shift freely in the blue sky
let them keep turning, like folding mats
let them change their skin from white to black
and form generous rain
we badly need
That's how it should be

Let the rain pour gently from the sky
let it pour when it's its turn
like never before
after the soil has been badly scourged
leaving our river a parched earth
let it pour and feed our dying crops
That's how it should be

Let the rain feed our only river
the emaciated river that can't move
let it flow and regain its full currents
so the fish can freely swim
so we shall not die of thirst
nor lack seafood
That's how it should be

And when the sun takes sway again
let it shine and dry topsoil
subsoil left moist and fresh
let it not fry our river again
let it spare our mourning crops
only helps them make their food
That's how it should be

Let the seasons show some kindness
let them come and go in peace
leaving behind joy, abundance, hope
taking nothing belonging to us
making us always want to watch them
as they take freely their turns
That's how it should be

Let's create our vision anew
so our frightful dreams may soon regain
their childhood sweetness
smiles and laughter beaming wrinkled
faces in deep sleep waking
greeted by sweet songs of songbirds
That's how it should be

16 July 2019

Green Campaign

(First published in *Dangerous Pastime*)

Enlightened rural children
Speak out against
Destruction of forests

Until
NGOs of the South
Enter into
Solar energy deals with
Companies
Overseas.

Can these
Organisations of green views
Not only widely distribute but
Train the rural communities
In its proper use in order
Not to
Undermine the need for
Energy
Saving and proper disposal?

16 September 2014

Save the Earth

(First appeared in *No Stress,* unpublished)

Put down those barrels,
Pick up your brains;
Don't go destroying,
Think of the future.
      Don't turn the forests
Into more deserts,
Spare lives and wildlife;
Secure our future.
      Do you know how long
It takes to bring back
A forest once dead?
Stop the destruction.
      Be innovative;
Create more new jobs
That bring in income
Without destruction.
      Let's use our great brains;
Create solutions
That give energy
Without pollution.
      Earth cannot take more
Of our pollution;
There is climate change
Threatening our own lives.
      We better think wise,
We better act wise;
No better warning
Than current warming.
      Seen ravaging tongues,
Raging storms and floods

Sweeping 'cross nations?
Earth needs no more stress.

31 August 2018

To Build Our New City

(First appeared in *No Stress*, unpublished)

Ignore complexity
Adopt simplicity
Avoid duplicity
Embrace tenacity
Even audacity

Bring new conviction
Backed by sure vision
With clear complexion
For sure completion
Of our construction

No more revision
Without compassion
Earning derision
But no compulsion
For its abrasion

Avoid delusion
Delete allusion
Go for precision
Shorten the session
Achieve the mission

With new alacrity
Avoid voracity
Promote humility
But not stupidity
To build our new city

15 May 2017

Trained Kleptomaniacs

Trained kleptomaniacs
Displaying such tactics

Celebrating megalomania
On coasts of Westamania

Nothing more excruciating
Than we going on emaciating

Sitting by foods so nourishing
In our forests flourishing

We eke out a living, carving
Nuts to circumvent starving

As kleptomaniacs so trained
Have left the forests drained

Come observe leaves relapsing
Just watch canopies collapsing

Come hear the roots crying
Come see the foliage dying

Stand not doing just praying
While they're all still playing

2 January 2021

Fed Four Billion Mouths

if truly it's you
that bore the burden
braved the sun
and tilled the soil
endured bruises
on your palms
sowed the seeds

if truly you did all that
and watered the forests and
it's we and they that came
to reap all ripe fruits
hanging on trees
of your profuse
drenching sweat

then stay quiet

if truly it's you, remain happy
beam your smiles
as you oft do
like the sun
every morning
give more hope but
keep yours too

if truly it's you, Mother Nature
still keeps your pay
a handsome package
as you've fed
four billion mouths
have kept their souls

from ever perishing

8 February 2021

Emotions

(First appeared in *Caught Between*, unpublished)

Tons of emotions
packed
in thoracic
canisters
pressure high
just waiting
for that moment
to explode
but
valve controllers
wise as they are
decide
to release these
in quiet
creative moments
producing
products that pacify
and sow seeds of peace
and sustainable development

1 August 2019

My Day

(First appeared in *Caught Between*, unpublished)

What a way
To start my day
What a great song
With a gong
A way
My day
A song
With gong
Like reading a book
By Akuren brook

What a ray
To light my way
What a crown
To dress my dawn
A ray
My way
A crown
On dawn
Like dancing on a beach
Men come to preach

18 August 2019

Wisdom

(First appeared in *Caught Between,* unpublished)

From the buccal cavity
of exposure,
it flows slowly,
sluggishly but steadily,
through the oesophagus
of readiness,
waiting for the right time,
when it's ripe
for ingestion
into
the chamber
of
experience
for easy digestion
by the enzyme of reflection into
that of deep knowledge
where it is absorbed
without
disturbance by
indigestion, constipation,
intermittent stomach aches,
or any such symptoms
ascribable
to overfeeding
or food poisoning,
into the bloodstream
of society
and ejected,
through the anal
canal of enlightenment,
into the farmland of
sustainable agriculture

for enrichment
of the humus soil
of collective endeavours
for use by all humanity,
solely
for the production
of healthy crops of the intellect
that benefit one and all,
to deserve
its uncommon name of wisdom.

11 August 2019

No New Ark

(First appeared in *Caught Between*, unpublished)

Destroy not the forests
Pollute not the atmosphere
No new ark for the second flood

15 August 2019

Green City

(First appeared in *No Stress,* unpublished)

Organic gardens
Like hanging Edens
Taking little spaces
Wearing some braces

See beautiful streets
Giving us some treats
Lined with trees and flowers
Green towers in showers

Look at great designs
Stop and read the signs
"Burn calories, not forests
Where men can take their rests"

Solar-powered houses
Inside, women in green blouses
Outside, waiting man in green suit
In green car producing no soot

At a table they all meet
Table set with less fish or meat
But more fruits and vegetables
Greeting vases with green pebbles

Now I see a truck
Obviously not stuck
But waiting for more trash
Without any squash

15 May 2017

Across Oceans

(First appeared in *Caught Between,* unpublished)

When big beams
of love flash
across oceans
and shared
unreservedly
abundantly,
with no strings
whatsoever attached,
instead of missiles of war
in harsh words
and hot balls of lead,
you can be sure
the blurring sky
will regain
it's bright blueness,
the paling soil
its dark brownness
and the browning leaves
their pure greenness.

27 October 2019

World Water Day

(First appeared in *No Stress,* unpublished)

Wonder not why tall, stunning Lady Fako, once dressed in a rich
forest skirt,
Our main source and supplier of generous fresh free-flowing water,
now
Rendered almost naked, displaying her desert headscarf
Let loose over her torn savanna blouse, now sends down stingy, trick-
ling
Drops to feed the multifarious pipes that run our homes and offices.

We here gathered today must think of astute ways to repair the
damage
And restore the natural beauty and integrity of Lady Fako, including
her sisters,
That once fed all and sundry generously with fresh free-flowing
water,
Entertaining no long queues at public taps that now receive hun-
dreds of frequently
Riotous crowds scrambling for what should have been flowing freely
at home.

Destruction by clearing and felling and burning of those green skirts
has led to this, and
All we need do is repair the damage now or run the risk of paying
the bitter price in
Years to come, when it will have been too late and more costly for
any repair to be done.

17 March 2018

Surface Warming

(First appeared in *No Stress*, unpublished)

Where huge mountains roll
And great rivers take their rise
There Eagles drive again to enrol
But en route the idea dies

Where forests form huge canopies
And insects make sonorous sounds
There no machines to make copies
Although IT today abounds

Where great lakes form a conjoint
And valleys create glorious armpits
Rapids doing the last bolt and joint
Crickets rising from the pits

Where all noises form a collective
Never again to rant apart
Every ranting done is selective
Each mouth playing a useful part

Where all silences now mellow
Into deafening wakening warning
Heard right from the deep below
Ripples rising for surface warming

Where parrots meeting in conference
Decide on who to clap and who to speak
Eagles flying over the confluence
But cautious not to crowd the peak

2 January 2017

Breaking Our Earth Apart

(First published in *Just a Bend*)

We always want to show off our great might
Prove our point to the rest of the world
Showcase military technologies, capabilities
And superior war skills, strategies and prowess
But we're, indeed, breaking our earth

We all share this one earth, our only planet
Yet with impunity, we send out missiles
Millions of miles away to test and prove
We've gone this far in this new craze with
Which we're shamelessly breaking our earth

The world needs far more than military might
Something that only makes billions live in fear
Hate and plans to revenge or start fresh attacks
When a billion live below the poverty line
While we're steadily breaking our earth

We've seen all these in wars on wars in terror
And can safely say nothing is new
Greatness must now be shown more in
Technologies hijacking wars and building peace
For we're seriously breaking our earth

Great nations should be those known with
More technologies to feed billions of mouths
To heal and bring more health to the world
Instead of pain and sorrow and soaring losses
As we're heartlessly breaking our earth

Our knowledge and skills and raw materials
To build what we now use to crack and break

We often get by cracking our earth
What a wonderful way of paying back
That we're now breaking our earth apart

10 June 2019

Change Climate Change

(First published in *Eni and Other Poems*)

Apply
With rigour
Polluters Pay Principle
Increase awareness
The storms are raging
Icecaps are melting
The seas are rising
Species are threatened
Send down the hammer
Cut down emissions
Reduce consumption
Switch to eco-technologies
Fade out your eco-footprints
Wake up to a bright new day
Help write the global anthem
Sing a new song for Mother Earth
Put out your lights in collective action
Join the fight to change climate change

2 March 2016

Share to Save the World

(First published in *Just a Bend*)

Don't be selfish
share every good thing in your head
share with others
share to save mankind

Those great skills you possess
show them at work to others
everything you've created
display for others to see and learn

You have good technologies
hide these not
transfer them to those in need
every new invention, share to save the world

17 June 2019

Dog's Desire

(First published in *Just a Bend*)

I need life
out of the cage, without a chain
away from the cold
out from under the table
sitting on the chair
dining at the table

I need
a soft and gentle touch
on my forehead
a warm hand
caressing my cheeks
a big hug of human love and care

17 June 2019

Even the Brave Fear the Wave

Look behind and beyond
at that seal and bond

that tear
apart even the rare

to find,
and see how blind

to the rivers of tears from that peak
torrentially coursing down the youth's cheek

you have been,
like a frozen seed of bean,

causing even the brave
to fear the wave.

14 November 2019

Your Care and Protection

We've been building our nests
on this tree without time for rests

We fly kilometres for palm leaves
missing catapult stones from eaves

We know they're children playing
but for our safety, we keep praying

We have built such wonderful homes
which you surely use as your tomes

We do all this and you simply copy
yet now you attack from root to canopy

We are so busy with our basic crafts
and never care to save the plan drafts

We if you without the drafts decimate
loss and impact you cannot estimate

We and neighbours produce samples
which you use and sell as examples

We then need your care and protection
not destroying us for self-projection

10 November 2019

A Child's Guilt

(Inspired by a childhood experience of Theophilus Ngwene)

I've been secretly following you
moving in and out of this house.
Doing what I didn't know.

Now I know! What a beautiful house
you've built on that wall in no time!
And I wish I could become as tiny as you

to join you and learn the secrets of your home and world.
But still human in form and reasoning. How many rooms
in there, to accommodate me? Because I'd like to have

a room to myself, as I'm tired of sharing this one
here where I currently live. I possibly will
figure out how to make myself tiny

enough to become part of your household and world.
But let me check first how many rooms there are
in there before I take the pain to reduce to your size.

Oh my, I didn't know it's so, so fragile.
And so loose, it's so easily dashed on the floor.
Ah, ah! I can't believe I've done this to you

before I've had the chance to talk to you
about my plan to join you and your community.
I can't believe I've so easily terminated your life!

What can I do to bring you back to life?
How can I repair this beautiful house of yours?
No, Mom, I can't eat, I simply can't!

See what I've done to this poor creature
whose house would have been my new
place of abode and learning. The house was right there,

and now it's right here in pieces on the floor. And
he's right here lying. Lifeless! And I feel so sad and guilty!
I cannot eat, Mom. Except you help me wake him up.

12 November 2019

Watch Out

Breathe the air
freely given
but listen to the message
of the breeze.

Use the water
generously supplied
but ignore not
the choking oceans.

Harvest the plants
and animals freely bred
and are at your service but
listen to the silent cry of Nature.

Open the bowel of the earth
for its precious minerals
but forget not
it could be empty one day.

Enjoy safe rides and travels
with your spouse and kids but
think of the future you're leaving
for the kids and their kids.

Enjoy life on earth
in its fullness
but watch out for signs
and causes of its destruction.
Watch out!

10 January 2020

Nature's Health

Stop the talk
Take a walk
Drop diction
Take action
Take a breath
Nature's health
You deserve
To preserve

14 January 2021

Done and Gone

When it's done,
It's gone;
May not easily
Be undone.

No need crying
Over spilt milk;
Over a broken egg,
Waste no time lamenting.

All you need do in such a state is
Support life meaningfully
In that irreversibility –
Call it The New Normal,

If you will –
Lest you drag it
Deeper into
A worse state;

When it's done,
It's gone;
Do well to avoid
A more regrettable state.

12 July 2020

Rivers of Conscience

We have walked
such a distance
and safely
are on the bank
of the river that has now trapped
our conscience.

Every molecule
strikes our conscience into consciousness
as it carries heavy loads
like the ones now on our minds
standing on its bank,
ready to cross.

Where are the fishes
that jumped up in mirthful display
when our presence they sense?
Where are the happy children
that enjoy their swims and
share in our delight to cross?

What the hell did we think
we were doing
emptying loads of pollution -
organics, chemicals, plastics -
into this river where now
our conscience is trapped?

To cross or not to cross;
to return home
walking that distance again;
to spend this time
picking up the garbage
floating its length and breadth?

Now in us flow
rivers of conscience,
in turbulence of meandering waves
and disturbing rhythm
harping on our senses,
waiting for our collective action.

8 November 2019

ACKNOWLEDGEMENTS

The motivation behind this collection was a request in September 2019 by Poetess Nnane Ntube who wanted to use my eco-poetry collection as one of the texts for her M.A. research. I realized that although I had eco-poems scattered in my several collections, I had no single volume dedicated to eco-poetry and decided to embark on this project.

Poems in this anthology span the 90s to 2021. While some of them were written in response to Nnane's timely reminder, others have been published in my previous collections: *Silent Voices, Death of Hardship, Dangerous Pastime, Eni and Other Poems* (Langaa Research and Publishing), and in *Just a Bend,* (Spears Media Press).

Some of the poems were still being developed and appeared in *No Stress and Caught Between.*

I'll like to thank my children who have spent a lot of time with me reading most of these poems and inspiring and encouraging me to continue writing: Okum, Arah, Beya, Offy, and Joy.

My late wife and friend, Eni Inyang, was a great source of motivation and support to me in my writing career, and I will always remain grateful to her. May her soul continue to rest in perfect peace.

Colleagues and partners in conservation, teachers, students and community members I have worked with since the 1990s, as well as some poets across the world have also been a great source of inspiration to me.

Scientists, it cannot be denied, have also influenced and inspired me somehow, and to them, I say thank you for the wonderful insights and breakthroughs aimed at helping us understand better how the earth works, what it faces and why, and how best to protect it.

It would be totally unfair if I failed to acknowledge the creatures

– from the tiniest to the biggest – out there in the wild, as well as those that live with and around us, for the great opportunity to learn from and be so inspired by them to write dozens of poems in this first anthology of eco-poems which I delightfully describe as The New Ark.

Finally, and more importantly, I thank the Almighty God for the skill, motivation and determination to come out with this anthology of eco-poems at a time when I was not only saddled with a lot of work but faced with a lot of challenges. To Him be the glory.

ABOUT THE AUTHOR

Credit: Courtesy of the author

Ekpe Inyang is a Chevening scholar and an award-winning writer with several scientific articles and textbooks to his credit in areas such as environmental science, environmental education, research methodology, socio-cultural forestry, and drama. He has distinguished himself as an accomplished playwright and poet, with eight published plays: *Professor Adoniah, Beware, The Sacred Forest, Water na Life, The Game, The Swamps, The Hill Barbers,* and *The Last Hope.* His published poetry collections include *Silent Voices, Death of Hardship, Eni and Other Poems, Dangerous Pastime, Just a Bend,* and most recently, *Tastes of Nature.*

As an educationist and environmentalist, Ekpe has made invaluable contributions to these fields, and has worked in different capacities with international organisations and institutions such as the Wildlife Conservation Society (WCS), World Wide Fund for Nature (WWF), and the Pan African Institute for Development - West Africa (PAID-WA). He is currently the Capacity Building Advisor and Education for Sustainable Development and Youth Empowerment Focal Point for WWF Cameroon.

Ekpe Inyang hails from the Korob (Korup) ethnic group in Ndian Division of the South West Region of Cameroon. He holds a Master of Science degree in Environmental Studies from the University of Strathclyde, United Kingdom.

ABOUT THE PUBLISHER

Spears Books is an independent publisher dedicated to providing innovative publication strategies with emphasis on African/Africana stories and perspectives. As a platform for alternative voices, we prioritize the accessibility and affordability of our titles in order to ensure that relevant and often marginal voices are represented at the global marketplace of ideas. Our titles – poetry, fiction, narrative nonfiction, memoirs, reference, travel writing, African languages, and young people's literature – aim to bring African worldviews closer to diverse readers. Our titles are distributed in paperback and electronic formats globally by African Books Collective.

Connect with Us: Go to www.spearsmedia.com to learn about exclusive previews and read excerpts of new books, find detailed information on our titles, authors, subject area books, and special discounts.

Subscribe to our Free Newsletter: Be amongst the first to hear about our newest publications, special discount offers, news about bestsellers, author interviews, coupons and more! Subscribe to our newsletter by visiting www.spearsmedia.com

Quantity Discounts: Spears Books are available at quantity discounts for orders of ten or more copies. Contact Spears Books at orders@spearsmedia.com.

Host a Reading Group: Learn more about how to host a reading group on our website at www.spearsmedia.com

Printed in the United States
by Baker & Taylor Publisher Services